A SOBER CELL: From the Inside Looking Out
©2022 Crystal Meth Anonymous

A

FROM THE INSIDE LOOKING OUT

SOBER
CELL

VOICES OF THE ®
FELLOWSHIP

TABLE OF CONTENTS

Foreword   5

Stories   9

   Inmate 6733457   11
   The Freedom I Found in Prison   17
   I Was Being Robbed   21
   Jail Prepared Me for This Journey   27
   A Lone Wolf   33
   Coming Full Circle   39

Start a Meeting   49

   Bringing CMA Inside a Facility   51
   Choosing a Meeting Type   52
   Basic Script Format   53

Our Readings   55

   What Is CMA?   57
   Are You a Tweaker?   59
   The Twelve Steps: A Plan of Action   61
   The Twelve Traditions   63
   I Can Stay Sober   65
   Today I Can   67
   There Is Hope   69

For More Information   71

FOREWORD

We, the members of Crystal Meth Anonymous, have worked diligently to put together this book for addicts who've been incarcerated. Many of us have been behind bars ourselves— so we've tried to design the book we wish we could have had. We believe these stories will give hope to anyone affected by crystal meth addiction, but we've compiled them particularly for those who are experiencing the challenge of being locked up.

These stories highlight the diverse backgrounds of CMA members, reminding us that addiction does not discriminate. The addicts represented here have very different histories, but they all share the same experience of serving time and finding recovery, in many ways as a direct result of the time they spent locked up. Most, if not all, of these fellows now give back by visiting prisons to carry the message to other addicts, truly coming full circle, as the title of the last story suggests.

There are Hospitals & Institutions committees in many cities where CMA is active, bringing the message of our program to addicts who are in facilities and can't attend outside meetings. They do this work gladly—it's incredibly fulfilling to help someone experience the shift in thinking recovery brings. Perhaps you'll begin being of service in a similar way by holding a meeting at your facility and providing support to fellow inmates who are looking for a way out of active addiction. We've included some of our readings and meeting formats in this book, so you can easily start a group and begin to build your own fellowship of recovering addicts on the inside. You can also reach out to us at crystalmeth.org or by using the mailing address at the end of this book to find more resources and communicate with people who can help you in your recovery.

In a day room, out on the yard, or sitting on a bunk—anywhere two or more addicts gather to talk about sobriety, a meeting can happen. A life free from crystal meth is just the beginning; soon, a whole new world can open up to you. We know it's possible because we've lived it, and we believe you can too.

STORIES

If you think you have a problem with crystal meth, you're in the right place. You always have a seat here. **Welcome home.**

INMATE 6733457

What a great day to be sober!

I used crystal meth, used it a lot, and found out that to continue using and continue paying for it, I'd need to do something drastic. So I learned how to do illegal things, and that's why you're reading this story.

I believe I came out of the womb addicted. I needed to find something that would stop the inner chat, the self-hatred. Something that would quiet me down and allow me to be who I was. Liquor was that remedy for me. Everything stopped. The world slowed down. That self-loathing voice, that questioning stopped, and everything got to be OK. Once I started, there was no way I would ever not drink again. That was at age 11.

I found other drugs and started to do pot and speed when I was still a kid. Back then they called it crank. It's a real dirty form of amphetamines. The bikers made it and hid it behind their crankshaft, so it was called crank. It was just wretched!

By the time I was 20, I'd already tried to get sober once and been arrested twice. I just wouldn't believe or accept that at my young age I was an addict or alcoholic. I'm a nice boy from a small town in New Jersey. That doesn't happen to people like me—that happens to bums and guys who sleep under buses and old people. That kind of thinking, and the discovery that I was gay, led me out again.

This time, "matchhead T" had made its way from California to New York—it was called Tina. What a love affair that was! When

I did my first bump of crystal, it was like everything I'd been searching for my entire life. I felt like the clouds parted, and the sunlight came out. My self-esteem was normal, if not elevated, my focus was directed, and I felt like I could do anything. Just like when I took that first drink at 11, there was no way I wasn't going to do it again.

People who know me know I am like a cheerleader. If I find something that works, I will shout it from the rooftops. I am a natural-born salesperson. So when I found the solution that fixed all my problems, I just had to tell everyone. I started to tell my friends, saying, "Let's get some." At first, it was kind of like Costco—the more you buy, the cheaper it is. When I was done splitting it up with my friends, I realized I didn't have to pay for mine anymore. I loved it!

I never thought this might be hurting my friends. I thought I was helping people! My friends told their friends, and pretty soon I was getting a lot of stuff. I decided to invest in a scale to make sure everyone was getting what they should. Pretty soon I was buying ounces and not thinking anything of it. I didn't even think it was illegal, because I wasn't doing it to make a lot of money.

Much later, when I got sober, I would say I was an "ethical moralistic drug dealer with convictions." I wouldn't cut the product, I'd sell good amounts, and I made sure it was good-quality stuff. Again, I honestly thought I was helping people.

I started to meet a lot of people involved in this lifestyle who were thieves, liars, and cheaters. It was like the musical *Little Shop of Horrors*—You don't meet good people on Skid Row. The more time I spent with these people, the more the people I thought I was helping got brushed aside. So when my friend of 12 years asked me to go out, I pushed him aside because I had to run my "business."

I became really cocky, going to FedEx and picking up pounds of crystal meth. That was insane. I would smuggle meth in Nilla wafer boxes I'd carry on the flight with me, even handing it to the guard as I walked through the metal detector. That's ballsy! That's addict behavior! That's the denial and grandiosity that come from having a chemically altered ego and a false sense of safety.

One day I got a call from one of the package carriers warning me that the DEA had just opened a package of mine and photographed it. To this day, I don't know who that was. I got scared and got rid of everything for a while.

But what was left when I got rid of everything was me. I had a need to get high. So one day a friend called, and I automatically ordered 2 pounds. I completely forgot that I was being watched, that my phone was being tapped, all of that. Because the need for more—for that sense of oblivion—was so great, I didn't even think twice.

I heard that my stuff was in, so I threw on my roller blades and plonked down four flights of stairs. As I put one blade to the ground outside, I was immediately grabbed by four or five different people and lifted off the ground and put in a van.

I didn't know what was happening. I thought I was being mugged again and yelled, "I don't have any money!" They said they were DEA, and I kept saying, "You got the wrong guy!" I actually didn't think I was that guy. I sat there forever. It was horrendous. They were grilling me for hours, a barrage of good cop/bad cop, and I kept saying, "You've got the wrong guy. You've got the wrong guy."

They asked if they could search my house, and I said yes. They didn't find much, but enough to arrest me. I remember being handcuffed to the chair in the "Tombs," a downtown holding cell, and just breathing and falling asleep. I guess subconsciously I thought, *This is over. Thank God, this is over*. When I came to, the cop said, "You know how I know you're guilty? The people who are guilty come in here and fall asleep."

People think recovery is a lot of work. For me, recovery is nothing compared to the amount of work I had to do to stay high. I think once I realized that the jig was up, that I no longer had to worry about going to sleep and having people throw stones at my window or ring my bell at all hours, that all that stuff was over, I was able to sleep and breathe.

So after spending six nights in jail without a shower or change of clothes, I got home and found they'd left a small vial of crystal in my destroyed apartment. Of course, I had to use it. I started my regular visits with the DEA and my lawyer, and through all of them, I was still getting high. I couldn't not get high.

The DEA began asking me to snitch, and I wouldn't, because I understood if I played the "game," I alone would reap the consequences—good or bad, I would go down alone. I'd say to them, "What do you want from me? I only got drugs for my friends, I'm not a dealer." They said, "You know, Mr. P., if you give drugs to someone, even if you don't charge them, you're a drug dealer—a bad drug dealer, but a drug dealer."

They couldn't get me for sales, but eventually they hooked me for possession and conspiracy. The judge hit me with all he could and gave me a sentence of three to life.

I was sent to prison. Guys in there would ask me what my bid was, and I'd tell them three to life. They'd ask, "Who'd you kill?" They'd say, "I shot four people, and I got three to six." Three to life is a long fucking time. I was only 34. It made me so angry. But I just kept putting one foot in front of the other, just trying to get out. I was Inmate 6733457, and I kept my head down.

One of my friends came to visit me in prison. He'd gone into recovery and brought me an NA Basic Text. When I looked at it, I was flooded with memories of my first foray into recovery, when I was 19. I'd forgotten all about the Twelve Steps, but when I opened up the book, I thought, *If I had only stayed in the program, I would have avoided all of this.* Today I realize I had to go through all of what I went through. I believe I have a Higher Power that's very gentle—sometimes too gentle. I needed to be kicked in the back of the head—my prison sentence—to realize I had to change.

So I stayed in my cell most of the time and read. I exercised and stayed healthy and kept doing the next right action, and three years went by pretty fast. I was able to go through a substance-abuse counseling system and get released.

When I was released, the counselor sat me down and said, "I have some advice for you: If you fail to plan, you plan to fail." He meant I needed to get to meetings. So when I got out, my friend took me to a Crystal Meth Anonymous meeting. There were a couple of people at the meeting I had used with. But they were different. They weren't messy anymore. They were totally different people. For one thing, they had their clothes on. They were able to speak in full sentences, and they didn't look like raccoons. This blew my mind. I thought, *If these people can do this, I should have no problem at all.*

There were so many attractive people in CMA at the time. The Traditions say that we're based on attraction rather than promotion. When I walked into the rooms of CMA, they were filled with such an attractive group of people that I wanted to come back every day. That's what kept me coming in the beginning, that and having no other friends and nothing much else to do.

Eventually, I started to hear my story and to feel like I was fitting in with people. I understood what they were saying and had something to share with them. These people were just like me; their thought process was my thought process. I couldn't find that anywhere else. Soon the attraction changed from physical to spiritual. I started to see how truly beautiful these people were inside.

This started my second journey into sobriety. I realized this time I couldn't do it my way. I couldn't go back to jail. No way! I had life on the back of my sentence. That means any violation— peeing outside, dirty urine, or getting in past curfew—and I was going back for two years at a clip. I decided I'd do whatever it took. Somehow it was easier at first, because I had that monkey on my back.

My parole officer called me one August and said, "You tested positive for marijuana." I said, "Absolutely not, it couldn't be!" She said she'd get back to me in a week. When I went to see her the next week she said, "You didn't test positive. I was just making sure you were stable. You're off parole."

In my mind I thought, *That's so messed up! What if I had gone out and used?* But what I learned is that no matter what, I was not going to get high.

Getting off parole was incredible, but it was scary and over-whelming. What was I going to have to keep me sober any-more? It wasn't until I talked to my mom that I realized how much it all affected me and how many intense feelings came up. Thank God for her! She was the one person I could show my true feelings to. I didn't have to put on a show and be a tough guy. I could freely weep like a baby and let it all out and be vulnerable.

My message to anyone reading this is that I didn't get high, and you don't have to get high either—ever again. For me, I had to do a lot of things to not want to get high. I needed to go to meetings, be of service, stay in contact with my Higher Power, work the Steps, have a sponsor and sponsees, and stay in reality.

Getting arrested wasn't fun, but today I think I was rescued, because I couldn't stop on my own. It started me on my path to the life I have now, which is completely unrecognizable to me and to the people who knew me. I get emotional when I talk about this, because I sometimes feel unworthy. The gift of this life and these people in recovery was given to me, and I'll be forever grateful. It's my obligation and honor and privilege to now extend the hand of recovery to others. I'm grateful to be sponsoring some great people right now—I can't even begin to count how many I've sponsored over the years. The funny thing about being a sponsor is the sponsee thinks you're helping them, but in reality, they're saving you.

I feel like Shelly Winters in *The Poseidon Adventure*. She swam to help all of the people get to safety, and then she drowned. So the deal is, I'm Shelly Winters, but I get to live. I'm able to reach out and guide and support all those who want to be saved. Maybe I can make someone smile, maybe I can make them feel safe, or maybe they can realize through my story that recovery is possible.

My program starts on a daily basis when I wake up and decide that I don't want to be Inmate 6733457. I want to be a productive member of society. We can lose the obsession to use drugs. If you're reading this thinking, *This isn't going to work for me— it's too much work, it's a waste of time*—I'm here to tell you it can, and it has happened for me.

THE FREEDOM I FOUND IN PRISON

I was never going to go to prison. My father went when I was 12 years old, and I wasn't going to be like him. I couldn't be like him. And as long as I wasn't like him, I could always justify that anything I did really wasn't that bad.

In my using career, I'd been arrested maybe a handful of times, spent a week in jail, and gotten a few misdemeanors. But nothing big enough to deter me from using. Nothing big enough to stop me from breaking into cars or stealing packages or doing all the other things that seemed like a good idea at the time. I felt like I was one lucky woman—I was invincible. Until I wasn't anymore.

When I got caught—and I mean really got caught—I was already on probation for possession. I had been faking my way through my UAs for two years. The day I was done with my probation was the day the criminal investigation into my extracurricular activities began. Within a few months, I'd be facing over 30 felony charges from three counties: identity theft, criminal trespass, misuse of a credit device, possession—the list went on and on and on.

I prayed a lot during this time. Not because I was particularly religious or spiritual, but because if there was some sort of divine being, I still felt like it owed me a favor. Even though I wasn't owed one, I still got one. My cases merged and overlapped, and after a year of courtroom appearances my felonies got pled down to just four and a deferred. I was even given the choice of prison or community corrections. Of course, I chose the latter. I figured it was a shorter route back to getting high.

Now, the next two years of my life went by in a blur at the not-so-therapeutic community I went to. Many of my days were spent staring at walls and wearing a stocking cap, a form of punishment they called "behavioral correction." It was a long two years, which I made longer by holding steadfast to my willful defiance. Eventually though, I made it to the outpatient part of the program.

This is where my story takes a not-so-unexpected twist. True to form and behavior, I kept pushing rules. Six months into OTC, one of my roommates reported that I'd applied for a credit card. This seemingly small act was the straw that broke the proverbial camel's back. That evening, I found myself in County on my way to finish my sentence behind bars. Something great happened that night, though. For the first time in years, I felt the anxiety that had been my constant state leave. I was still scared to go to prison. You hear stories that create an image in your mind—expectations, questions, fear. The reality usually exists somewhere between these things.

Two weeks later I was settled at my final facility, a women's medium-security. As strange as it sounds, this was the first time I'd been able to really breathe in over two years. I'm not saying that prison was fun, but no one yelled at me, I wasn't in constant fear, and no one made me sit staring at a wall for weeks on end. I'm probably one of the few people who can say they felt freer in prison than they did before, but it's true.

My sentence went by quickly, in retrospect, but it didn't seem so at the time. However, as hours and days melted into weeks and months, and one year rolled into the next, that I was busy became my saving grace. I was on a work crew that got loaded up in a van six days a week in the summer to go do manual labor. We planted, weeded, and harvested fields. It was hot and hard work, and sometimes we came back to the unit covered head to toe in mud. But I got to put my hands in the dirt every day. Sometimes we even got to put a ripe, freshly pulled tomato on our bologna sandwiches. A tomato, something I'd taken for granted my whole life, became the most delicious thing I ever tasted. In the winter we went out a few days a week and ran chainsaws and stacked wood. There was an understanding on the crew: Everyone pulled their own weight. We just did.

On the days we didn't go out or when a meeting or appointment kept me in my unit, I fed my brain and spirit. I was connecting to something in those fields every day, and I wanted to find out what. So I read everything the library had on spirituality, physics, history, and cultures of the past. I didn't go into the yard too much, because I wanted to avoid a write-up at all costs. I was set to get out early and chose to pass much of my time by myself rather than risk spending extra time inside. I read and I watched TV and I met with the chaplains and went to programs sometimes, but my stretch was mostly boring. I made almost no friends inside—I didn't want to get pulled into drama. Yeah, it was boring, but I got my earned time.

The night before I got out, I didn't sleep at all. I feared some mysterious last-minute force was going to keep me in there. But it didn't happen, and I did eventually get to leave. My two-year tail was just as boring and uneventful as my stay in prison, aside from an initial relapse I ended up confessing about to my parole officer. The whole time I was on parole, I followed every rule. I called and left a message if I was going to be two minutes late for curfew and was overly thorough in getting permissions beforehand. My parole went on for a few extra months because the office forgot I existed. I didn't have a single violation; they had no reason to know who I was.

My first CMA meetings happened before I went to prison. I even had a sponsor, but I just half-assed my Steps, doing them so I had a "look good" for my program. The smart thing to do after getting out of prison would have been to go back to the support I had at CMA. But why would I do that? Instead, I let fear, my desire to be "normal," and a pair of blue eyes convince me I didn't need meetings. After all, I white-knuckled it through my parole. Surely this meant I was cured.

The day I was off parole, I was high. It wasn't meth, and it was legal, so it was OK. That's what I told myself. Of course, to go with my weed I needed booze. Then, when Blue Eyes got off paper some months later, we had to celebrate with some coke. In a few months it was nightly drinking, pills, powders, and a whole plethora of "whatcha got?" As long as it wasn't meth, it was no big deal, right?

Big shocker: Blue Eyes and I broke up just over a year later. I was free now. Since he was the problem, the bad influence, it stood to reason that if I only did legal substances, everything would be fine. But I still felt empty. I had to drink and smoke weed to numb myself. And I had to drink more and smoke more when it stopped giving me the effect I wanted. One night, after a regrettable liaison with a guy I barely knew, I found myself asking a question I should've asked long ago: "What the hell are you doing?" I had no answer. I didn't know. In that moment, I realized that I was just as lost as I had been my whole life.

Searching for direction, or maybe to prove I was hopeless, I went to a meeting the next day. And I went to one the day after that and the day after that. Then I got a sponsor, and I actually did my Step work. I wasn't always happy about it, especially when I had to confess a secret that had been poison in my veins, but I did it because I didn't know what else to do.

It would be impossible to pinpoint exactly which Steps made me feel less hopeless and which ones allowed me to like myself. But, by the time I was through all twelve, I was able to look at myself in the mirror without hating who was looking back. When I started doing service, that self-like turned to self-love, and my ego made way for selflessness. I have found everything I ever wanted in CMA: friendship, purpose, connection, and the ability to love myself. Most important, I don't want to get high anymore. I just don't think I'd enjoy it. Not when I have so many other things to look forward to.

I did end up going back to prison years later—as a volunteer. The guards and staff remembered me, probably because I had always been civil to them, and my application went through in a week. I get asked a lot if it's weird going into the prisons I was once at, and my answer is usually the same: "Only the first time." All these years later, when I walk through the gates and hear the clunky sound of the metal doors opening and closing, I'm not filled with dread. And I'm not filled with fear. If anything, I am honored that I get to be proof that a prison sentence doesn't have to determine what a person does with their life after they get out. I do a lot of service for Crystal Meth Anonymous now. But my volunteer work in the prisons will always hold a special place in my heart. It shows me just how far I have come.

I WAS BEING ROBBED

The man in my house was robbing me. I ran down the street and banged on a neighbor's door. No one answered. Another door. No answer. And another. No answer. *Why aren't they answering me*, I thought. *I am being robbed!*

Finally, the cops came, thank God.

While doing their job clearing and securing my house, the police found drugs and paraphernalia. They began talking to the other man in the house and heard his side of the story. They decided to take both of us to the station to sort everything out. Once we arrived, he went into one room and I went into another. For some reason, one of my hands was cuffed to a bench. I was confused about this and demanded an answer.

"Why are you doing this to *me*?"

Little did I realize, at the time, they were restraining me because they'd been called about a man with a gun. How did the police know to come? The man robbing my house had called them. Why didn't he just leave? He couldn't—I'd slashed three of his tires.

Why? Because. I had a Winchester .30-30 rifle in one hand and a bayonet in the other. It was 5:30 on a Sunday morning, and I was running up and down the street in South Philly with no shirt or shoes on, stark raving mad after being awake for four days high on crystal meth.

I was in that room cuffed to the bench for what seemed like hours, getting madder and madder and yelling at the cameras in the ceiling. Eventually, four cops came into the room. I will never forget the next words out of their mouths:

"Sir, you are being charged with..." They read a list of eight or nine charges against me. Still in manic disbelief, I resisted the truth.

"What, are you kidding me? *I was the one being robbed!*"

After the embarrassment of being fingerprinted, my hands, feet, and waist were fully shackled. Then the mugshot. With that shameful flash of the camera, I flashed back 15 years. I'm having my picture taken in my Army Class A military uniform. I looked good and felt great in that uniform. I was in top physical condition and at the peak of my career. Within a few years, I'd retire from the Army as a Sergeant First Class after 20 years of proud service to our country. I'd marched in Memorial Day parades. I was *revered* at my local VFW.

And now, I'm being shuffled into a courtroom for an arraignment—an emaciated, strung-out mess with insane delusions.

As I faced the judge and the charges were read out loud in a courtroom filled with strangers, I began crying my eyes out. The court officer read about terroristic threats, possession of weapons with intent, involuntary servitude, false imprisonment, simple assault, criminal mischief, possession of a controlled substance, and possession of drug paraphernalia. The reality of the situation finally started to register, and my denial and disbelief gave way to horror. I was going to jail, and I wanted to die.

I was stripped of my civilian clothes, got the cavity search and a medical exam, then had my intake into the jail. I was given a suicide suit crudely named the turtle suit, which was nothing more than a large piece of padded material with Velcro strips on it, designed to keep me from hurting myself. This of course meant I was headed to the psych ward. The handcuffs went back on, and I was assigned a cell. As I was shuffled down the hallway, the Velcro on the turtle suit wouldn't stay fastened and it began falling off me. Here I am, with a bunch of strangers in a jail watching me stumble half-naked down a hallway toward my waiting cell.

Once the door shut and locked behind me, overwhelming exhaustion set in. The lights were on all day and night, 24/7—I was on a suicide watch. I could only muster enough strength to get up and get my food at the cell door when it came. I felt total despair—how was I ever going to get out of this situation? My life had become so twisted and distorted. Thoughts of my family flashed through my still-racing mind. I'd burnt every bridge I ever had with them as it stood. Suicide seemed like an answer, but, frankly, I was so broken and hopeless I couldn't even manage trying that. Besides, I was being monitored by the guards around the clock.

I have no idea how long I was in that cell. Was it a few hours? A few days? I just don't know, and at the time I didn't care. Eventually, someone banged on my cell door—the ward psychiatrist. He was there to see his newest patient. We briefly talked about my condition and care; then he told me he'd be back tomorrow, and we'd talk some more. His manner was firm but not ugly, on guard but not combative. In the midst of my despair, I at least felt like I had someone and something to look forward to, his daily visit. As alone as I felt, I had an ally, even though I didn't feel like talking to him or anyone else. I barely wanted to be around myself.

There were other inmates who were assigned to watch me through the slitted window of the cell door to make sure I didn't try to hurt myself. After a few days of detoxing, I slowly started to talk to my babysitters, as they were called. They conveyed to me how to survive in jail. First, be responsive and respectful to the guards on duty. I stayed humble; I was deferential to my babysitters and the guards. Second, act like I was part of life again. The quicker I did so, the quicker I'd get regular jail clothes instead of the turtle suit. I made my bed, cleaned my cell, and stayed alert. The fog started to lift, and before I knew it I was taken off suicide watch by the psychiatrist, which meant I was given regular jail clothes. Definite progress.

As I sobered up, one fearful thought nagged at me: What would happen when people in my neighborhood heard what I'd done? How was I going to look my friends and neighbors in the eye again without shame?

It was breakfast time the morning after I came off suicide watch. The cell door opened. In stepped a guard. "Do you know who I am?" he asked. "No," I replied.

He proceeded to identify himself. He was one of the volunteer firefighters who knew me from marching in the Memorial Day parades. As soon as I placed him, I was horrified at the thought that there was a guard working in this godforsaken jail who knew me. He was someone from my neighborhood. That over-whelming feeling of fear and shame just gripped me. Tonight he might be gossiping about me at the very VFW I marched for. But sitting in jail, I could do nothing about it. Little did I know—my story had already been covered by the local newspapers. What was done was done. And I had done it.

I was no stranger to the judicial system, by any means. I'd racked up several DUIs over a 20-year period and knew the system well. The usual sequence for me always went like this: jail, lawyers, money, summons, hearing, rehabs to appease the courts, pro-bation and fines, then back on the streets. But this time it was different. Thanks to the keen eye of the psychiatric staff, a miracle happened. The doctor saw something in me that I'd never real-ized was there. While trying to interview me about my military history, he noticed I'd become very withdrawn and silent.

After a couple of sessions, he asked me, "Do you know what PTSD is?"

I said, "I've heard of the term before, but I'm not sure just what it is."

"I think you have it," he said and began to explain to me what post-traumatic stress disorder was. "You don't need to be in a jail," he said. "You need psychiatric help."

That diagnosis afforded me a bed at an Army medical center. While there at the rehab, I met other vets who had some of the same problems and symptoms I was having. In therapy, I described how the smell of burnt oil or plastic would trigger severe memories of my combat experiences. I'd immediately have this overwhelming feeling of fear and want to flee wher-ever I was. I'd isolate at home and drink. Most of the time, I just drank to pass out. I didn't want to dream; I wanted to suppress the nightmares and recurring thoughts of war.

When I went to AA, I could relate, to some extent. Alcohol was my first love, but once I ventured into crystal meth use, it took precedence. When I found crystal, I thought I'd found my best friend. The speed allowed me to stay up for days, bypassing sleep and the nightmares, night sweats, and panic attacks. I was hooked. I already knew the consequences of meth use from meeting addicts at earlier rehabs, but I chose to do it anyway. I gradually gravitated to CMA because I could relate more to what was being shared there—the things I was hiding from, the paranoia, seeing people and things that weren't really there. I could relate to all these things. It seemed like CMA dealt more with what was going on in my life. I felt like I had a home.

In CMA one of the topics we talk a lot about is sex and how much a part of our using it was. In AA they didn't talk about all the places the drugs took us. The "I'll never do that" stuff—lying to friends and trying all sorts of things I'd never do on alcohol, because I wanted crystal more than I wanted alcohol. In CMA we go into that in depth.

It wasn't until I was ready to let go of my past that the psychiatrist and I could really work through the pain. I had the choice to suppress the information and shortchange myself in the long run; but his interest and compassion outranked my insanity and insecurity.

After a few months in the Army hospital, I left and truly started my journey in recovery. I attribute the work I did there and the work I'm doing today as a key to my sobriety. The worst part of jail was the sitting and waiting—waiting for food, showers, visits from anyone, staff or relatives; waiting for that door to open even to be in the communal area; waiting to be able to just interact with others. But for me, that one relationship I made with the psychiatrist was the one my spirit needed to awaken, so I could truly start to live. I've come a long way from sitting in that shithole in South Philly and eating condiments for breakfast, lunch, and dinner because I'd spent all my money on drugs.

The best part of jail was the camaraderie among some of the staff and other inmates. I learned that I am not alone—ever. That we need one another. That I can feel a connection to another human being, even under desperate circumstances.

Once I reentered society, I started going to fellowship meetings at a local community center to continue working on my alcoholism. It was at this center one day that I noticed another group letting out just before ours.

"What meeting is that?" I asked a fellow.

"CMA, Crystal Meth Anonymous," he replied.

I needed to find out more about this meeting. After all, it was crystal that landed me in jail and brought me to my knees. I attended the next meeting. At my very first one, I knew I was home. For the first time in my life, I could relate to people. I felt safe. So I made it my home group.

After going to several meetings and listening to what people were saying, I found a great sponsor. Someone I felt comfortable with and could relate to. I thought I was unique, and nobody was like me or would understand me. But once I found this sponsor, I discovered that I wasn't unique and that we all were sent down the same dark path. He could relate to the paranoia, the sex drive, and the insanity. This made my recovery easier—just to be able to talk about things I didn't think I could tell anyone about. Me, this big burly military guy! My sponsor was able to tell me I wasn't as unique as I thought I was. He pulled things out of me I thought I couldn't express to anyone before, the things I was too ashamed to tell anyone.

After getting a sponsor, I got right to work on the Twelve Steps and threw myself into service. I try to help others who still suffer from crystal meth addiction. I have sponsees I'm taking through the Steps. I find that to be the most rewarding part of my sobriety. Now I live one day at a time and stay in service, helping the newcomer who's struggling. I try to take as many commitments as I can. I started off by doing service at my home group, and then at the VA hospital. I took some commitments, told my story for Hospitals and Institutions, and then branched out into other roles, like H&I chair and serving as delegate for our area.

I've learned how to guide people to sober houses and halfway houses. I gathered a network of recovery friends, which allows me to understand I no longer need people, places, and things from my past. A lot of young people got out of rehab and are afraid to talk about it. I can tell my story and make them feel like they're among friends who understand. I stay plugged in with the vets and the VA hospital.

I still feel like I have a lot of work to do. I'm not going to walk around like I know everything, because I don't. I don't want to ever think that I "have this"—I don't. I'm just one drink or drug away from losing everything: my recovery, my family, and my dreams.

It's been over four and a half years since that horrible morning. Today, I look back at that life I'd been existing in, not living in. No more. Today, I live one day at a time.

JAIL PREPARED ME FOR THIS JOURNEY

It was the night before I took my plea. I'd been arrested four months prior for my first felony charges, and, with the reluctant help of my father, I'd hired a lawyer who was going to get me a deferred judgment and probation. The deferred judgment would be sealed, effectively allowing me to put my unfortunate life of meth behind me. I just had to show up and not be high.

Oh, the trouble with doing simple tasks while on meth! I told myself I'd stop using three days before my court date, but the night before I was so high, the abscessed tooth I'd been ignoring became excruciating, and my friend and I were pulled over with drugs in the car on our way to the hospital. The police ran our IDs, realized who we were, made an excuse to search the vehicle without our consent, and found the drugs. And we were arrested with new felonies.

I'd been arrested and gone to jail twice before on minor offenses and been easily bonded out by my mother or friends. I remember standing in the Sallyport (the garage entrance to jail), handcuffed and ashamed of my first felony arrest, and swore confidently that I'd never be in this miserable place again. Little did I know I'd be there a dozen more times, having been picked up on warrants or new charges.

I'd only been to the Denver City Jail up to this time and never for more than a day or the weekend. That's where you go if you'll be bonded out quickly or are waiting to be transferred to another facility. My new arrest and third felony charge ensured I'd be transferred to County Jail with a bond of $50,000. I wasn't going anywhere anytime soon.

The fear of what waited for me at County was all-consuming, and during a bed check the guards found me doing the squirrel dance in my cell in the middle of the night. They asked if I was all right, and in a foolish moment of honesty I said, "I don't know." Jails are not equipped to handle psychiatric issues, and if you're not all right, you're viewed as suicidal and a protocol is implemented.

I was stripped, provided a weighted vest, and put in a cell by myself with a plexiglass door in full view of all the male and female sheriff's deputies for monitoring. I tried to sleep, but the cries of another inmate—he'd refused to vacate his cell and subsequently broke his arm in a scuffle with the deputies—kept me wide awake. It was 3:00 a.m., and the doctor wouldn't be on to assist him for another five hours.

At 7:00 a.m., I was clothed and handcuffed, had my legs shackled, got handcuffed to another inmate, was loaded onto a bus, and was driven with 60 other men to County Jail. It was only 8 miles from downtown, but you might as well be in another country. The clang of the metal door behind us marked the seriousness of our collective future.

After processing, I was put into a large open room called a pod with 80 men in bunk beds. There was no room for me and the other new arrivals, so we were put into "boats," plastic kayak-shaped beds in everyone's way in the middle of the room. I tried to sleep and not think about what trouble I was causing while people openly grumbled and cursed as they had to make their way around us.

Most of the people there were career criminals on their way to prison. Despite being 35 at the time, I was a boy among men. I was petrified. Nothing in my past had prepared me for this experience.

I pleaded with my mother, 2,000 miles away, on a collect phone call to bail me out, but she refused. She confided that it helped her sleep at night knowing where I was and that I was alive. She hadn't been able to say that for years. Regardless, I was furious. I felt abandoned. I couldn't believe she'd let this happen to me.

With no other choice, I fell into the routine of life in the pod. During the waking hours, the room was filled with a din that was inescapable.

Having a head clear of drugs for the first time in years provided the motivation to make some changes. I walked around the pod for an hour three times a day. I wrote letters to family and friends while others watched TV. I attended classes on anger management, as I certainly exhibited a shortage of it there. I also attended some Twelve Step meetings regularly. My mother sent me some books, and for the first time since college I read for pleasure.

Periodically, I'd be summoned to court by being woken up early in the morning and told to get dressed. I'd get shackled and transported by bus to the court house, where I'd be paraded through the halls handcuffed to three other prisoners like a chain gang, sit for hours in a cramped holding cell, see the judge for a few minutes, go back to the holding cell, and then be bused back to County Jail in the late afternoon. It would take about 13 hours, completely demonstrating the process of hurry-up-and-wait while instilling a feeling of entire helplessness.

After trips to court, we'd sometimes return to jail too late for chow. In these situations, we ate by ourselves in the mess hall, served sack lunches of baloney sandwiches with packets of ketchup (yes, ketchup!) and a warm container of milk. On one such occasion, after I'd been in County for a month and a half, I opened my bag and discovered, to my surprise, that I'd been given a Chinese mustard packet. I knew the kitchen had mustard—they just didn't serve that with baloney as one more F.U.—but Chinese mustard? One of the inmates who'd been handcuffed to me all day jumped up and exclaimed, "That's a sign! You're getting out!" We all had a good laugh about that.

The next morning the deputy on duty yelled my name and the most satisfying words I'd heard in 50 days: "Pack it up!" I was being released. How about the power of that mustard! My excitement was contagious. People crowded around my bunk and helped me pack. They asked me to reach out with mes-sages for friends and family on the outside. I was wished well with my new sobriety, and we were all brimming with confi-dence that I was past this tragic chapter of my life. My "new leaf" was waiting to be turned, and away I went to begin the discharge process.

But a month later I was back. Stunned and disheartened, I tried to figure out what had happened. I had managed to stay clean for a week, but I couldn't find a job with three pending felony charges. A friend (a fellow dealer) offered to pay me to just deliver some drugs to customers for him, but that lasted only a few days before I asked to be compensated in meth rather than cash. I missed a UA and an appointment with my probation officer and was on the run, until I was picked up on the resulting warrant.

A cycle of getting out, trying a new way to use while on probation, failing miserably, and going back to jail ensued. This ate me to the core, and it seemed nothing would change, except going to prison. A string of new felony charges and an indictment did just that. The DA recommended I serve the 12 years associated with my original felony charge. I was sent back to jail to wait for prison to pick me up. That night, lying in my bunk with the weight of the world pressing against me, I had a moment of clarity.

I realized I'd been living in fear of every aspect of my life, and my answer in any situation was to get high. I'd finally figured out my problem now that it was too late.

A week later it was a friend, not prison, who came for me. He bonded me out of jail. This was not a small feat. He had to pay $2,000 cash. He said he wanted help with his business and felt I would be invaluable. Actually, he really needed my skills as a dealer, so he could have a steady supply of meth while he ran his business into the ground. I found him drugs, and while walking to his home, I swore to myself I would not use.

One night, we were both high sitting around his place, but for the first time in my life, the drugs didn't do what I needed them to do: stop my mind from telling me I am a piece of shit and I deserve every bad thing I have coming to me. I was frantic. I was scared. I left and walked home, freaking out the whole way. The next morning, another friend called and asked if I wanted to go to a meeting.

I had no excuse. I agreed, and I've been here ever since. I was able to arrest my erratic behavior and replace the need for drugs with a need for Twelve Step recovery. I worked on my program while I prepared for what seemed the inevitable trip to prison looming on the horizon.

I found a home in the fellowship of Crystal Meth Anonymous. Meetings, sponsorship, and service work became a part of my daily life. I found work and saved for the cost of an attorney. Even though I was getting better, I was still me. I did have to go to jail once for missing a court date through carelessness with my schedule. I was sober and had some means of addressing my own problems. I called my employer to let him know what had happened. I had some money and was able to bond myself out, so I only had to be in for a weekend. This was a valuable lesson in accountability.

I shared often in meetings about my legal situation and the fear it brought. People would try to encourage me by saying, "You can carry the message in prison." That wasn't comforting at all. I didn't want to go. My sponsor continually reinforced the idea of living life on life's terms. This meant accepting whatever happened and knowing I would be all right regardless. I regularly prayed to my Higher Power to prepare me for the journey.

Eight months later, I appeared in court ready for whatever was in store. That same DA had been observing me from a distance without me realizing and knew I'd made a change for the first time. He changed his recommendation from prison to probation, and the judge agreed. I have enjoyed continuous sobriety since my first meeting. And I haven't been to jail again either.

I'm fortunate—jail allowed me to hit bottom at just the right time. Many do not get that chance or don't recognize it when it's happening. I would never have admitted it before, but jail saved my life.

A LONE WOLF

My early years and childhood were a confusing mess. I am the youngest child of three; my older brothers were seven and eleven years older than me and from another marriage. My mother and father didn't get along, and both had challenges within themselves. I now understand that they did the best they could with what they had, but I was left with an aggressive, abusive father and an emotionally distant mother. Through this chaos, I always felt like a lone wolf without a home. My parents divorced when I was 11, and a chaotic home life developed which pushed me further into the loner-who-doesn't-fit-in mind-set.

That year, I started partying with my friends, smoking cigarettes and drinking pretty hardcore. The whole goal was to get as drunk and have as much fun as possible. We'd run around town acting like fools. We certainly blacked out a lot and had a lot of problems, but at that point it was extremely fun and an escape from life in general. Soon we found marijuana and started to live the stoner life, throwing parties in all available places. School became the lowest priority until, one by one, we all dropped out. Our parents weren't capable of caring for us or holding us accountable at this point.

We began partying harder and dealing drugs. As 13-year-olds, we thought we had figured out the key to success—we were living like all of our heroes. And living like that led us directly to crystal meth. It started out simple, doing it once in a while at a party. But soon the time between use started to shrink and so did our care about any other substances.

From this point, we began to live the "crew" life, where a bunch of us misfits cliqued up and dreamt of building a big enterprise from hustling. We started off small—minor thefts, mostly from stores. But we proceeded to get more insane and do wilder stuff. This truly was the fun time of addiction, if there ever was one. While there were consequences, they were minor, like getting kicked out of school or stopped for shoplifting—nothing major in our eyes. Throughout this time, we'd see a lot of people get in trouble and go to prison for long periods. We thought we were different. That would never be us! We were smarter, and we certainly didn't have a problem. It was a wild, fun time to be alive.

At 19, it all came crashing down. Major consequences began to rear their ugly heads as a result of my crystal meth addiction. I was arrested and indicted on pretty serious weapons charges. The whole process of being put in a cop car, sent to the police station, and handcuffed to a wall while they tried to rattle me wasn't enough to jar something loose and make me think I had a problem. No, I was delusional, thinking I hadn't done anything wrong, and it was someone else's fault. I got long-term probation. I quickly violated it and went on the run.

They caught up with me quickly. My probation was revoked, and they sentenced me to a year in County Jail. To make matters worse, the jail was in the Arizona desert, living in tents in 100-plus-degree temperatures. But again, I rolled in thinking I did not have a problem; it was someone else's fault. Quite honestly, at the time it felt like a rite of passage; all of my heroes in the game had been to jail or prison. I had finally arrived! When I got to my housing, I sat back and surveyed the land.

From there I began to hang out with the influential crowd and ran around—still acting like a fool—trying to be somebody in jail. There was talk of a reduced sentence if I took a drug rehabilitation program, so I jumped at it, though I still didn't think I had a problem. I rolled into this program like a true tough-guy convict. I didn't take it seriously, told them what they wanted to hear, joked around, and judged everyone. When it came time for people to lead Twelve Step meetings, I made fun of the Steps and the people and cracked jokes about how lame it was. Even though I didn't take it seriously, somehow I passed through. Little did I know the judge put the "dangerous" tag on me, so I wasn't eligible for a reduction of my sentence. But time ticked away, and I finally got released.

When I got out, I picked up right where I left off, like I hadn't even been gone for an extended period. I was right back in cuffs again in less than a year on some serious charges, all as a result of my actions while using crystal meth. This time, I lost three and a half years of my life, and they promoted me from jail to the Department of Corrections and prison.

Again, I did not have a problem, just some bad luck. (And a bad choice of friends, who told on me.) I rolled into prison like a king, repeating the process. I'd survey the land, find out where I fit in, and do my time. I got tired of lockdown one day and asked to go to a Twelve Step meeting, just to get out of my cell. When I got there, they had the Steps on the wall, and honestly, nothing like recovery was spoken about. Or if it was, I was shut off to what I thought was ridiculously useless. I kept hearing "Power Greater" and "God," and in my head I thought, *What is this, some science fiction junk?* To me there was no God, because if there was, surely He would have managed my life a lot better and I wouldn't be in prison. Right?

I rode my time out, not thinking I had a problem at all. Since I didn't have anyone who wanted to take me in for parole, I had to do all of my time. But I got out and picked up right where I left off with some different faces and a lot of crystal meth and violence. Again, I did not make it on the streets a full calendar year but was in handcuffs and stripes once more, going through the jail and court process, hoping it wasn't as bad as my public defender was telling me. But it was bad, and I lost two and a half more years of my life in prison. This time, I started to realize I had a problem. I didn't know exactly what that problem was, but I had one. Was it my family, the police, alcohol, drugs, crystal meth? My life was such a train wreck, I couldn't pinpoint it.

I changed the way I approached my time and began to work on myself, reading, doing college classes, running, and working out. I set a plan for my life. This whole time I had been a lone wolf, with no signs of love from the world. No one came to visit me. I never got mail. I can vividly remember mail call and seeing everyone happy to get letters and pictures. Inside I felt hurt, but I couldn't show that weakness in prison, so I turned it into acting pissed off all the time. But now I wanted that calm square life of a job, house, family, etc. So I made a plan for how to get that life. I thought I had all of the answers and a bullet-point plan to get there. I was released to a halfway house.

Being in that halfway house blew my mind. We had to wake up early for morning reflection and work, and then we had to do a Twelve Step meeting at night. And again, they were big on this God thing. I laughed and thought how lame it was. *That's just the answer for weak people. That won't work for me.* So again, I acted like it didn't matter, played the game, and tried to follow my plan. But when my plan fell apart, I took off. I left with every intention of not getting loaded. I wasn't going to screw this up. But after a few days, I ended up in that black hole, a place filled with chaos and turmoil and feelings I knew nothing about. So I went back to my friend alcohol, who led me back to crystal meth and running and gunning.

At this point, I really knew I had a problem, but I had no solution or help. So I started to scramble. I went to six halfway houses in as many months, but I'd leave in the middle of the night whenever that black hole hit me. I did the same at three detox facilities in three months. None of this was working. I couldn't escape the black hole. My last chance was rehab, but that black hole followed me, and I left after six days.

I caught a minor charge after this and had to do 10 days in jail. I remember going in high and getting to my bunk. As I got my bunk set up, I heard over the speaker "Crystal Meth Anonymous meeting in the meeting room." I had never heard of CMA, but I knew I had a problem with speed, so I went. When I got there, it was not what I expected. I had been to many institutional Twelve Step meetings, and they all seemed stuffy and lame. But this one was led by two people who seemed cool and knew what they were talking about. They didn't talk on and on about God; they talked about how the program of CMA taught them how to be good men and stop being convicts who were in and out of prison. I liked this, but I was still skeptical. I went once more, and it was the same experience. They talked to me and treated me like a human being, not a convict.

I got out of jail not wanting to get loaded, but I did. I was 28 years old with nothing to show for my adult existence. The longest I'd held a job was for two months. The longest relationship I had with a human being was for six months. I was living in a beat-up car. I had three restraining orders, two from family members and one from my ex-girlfriend. Just like a good tweaker, I had a spot where I could park my car and plug an extension cord into a building. I could plug my space heater in during winter and put cardboard up over the windows and proceed to get loaded on meth, hoping to obliterate my feelings.

At this point, in my loaded state, I took stock of my life. I'd been locked up three times, tried halfway houses, detox, and rehab. I thought I'd actually tried a Twelve Step program, and I thought I had tried God, because I did a lot of foxhole prayers. I thought being in prison was going to be my life plan. In that car, I had an epiphany: I did not want to get high anymore! I'm not sure if you can relate to this, but with my whole being, I did not want to get high. But my arm would not stop bringing the pipe to my lips. If you have ever cried your eyes out while getting high, you know the powerlessness I am talking about. Hope was gone. I decided right then and there to kill myself. Obviously, I failed that mission. But I remember vividly that the thought of suicide gave me hope. I made it through the night, but something had changed. My main focus was to get back into rehab and give it an honest shot.

As I was settling in at rehab, they announced a CMA meeting, which made me happy. I got into that meeting. The chair had invited a speaker. He was someone I'd seen at a CMA meeting in jail. To me, that was more than a coincidence, and the first sign I'd gotten that a power greater than myself was pulling some strings to get my attention. When I heard the speaker talk, he looked like a professional businessman but spoke like a tweaker. When he told his story, he did so in a way that made me believe he knew what he was talking about, had been where I was then, and had found a way out.

I walked up to him and asked him if he would sponsor me. That I did that freaked me out. I was a grown man who didn't need another judge, probation officer, CO, or DO. He said yes and proceeded to meet with me in rehab. He didn't talk about God, but about how his life was and how it is now, which helped build the relationship of trust.

Once I got out, I began hanging out with that man. We just relaxed and did cool stuff while doing Step work. He proceeded to take the book that contains the Twelve Steps and trans- lated it from what seemed like a foreign language. From there things started to take off. I gave the program my all and did what people asked of me. It seemed like the more I focused on the program of recovery, the more positive things happened in my life.

As of the writing of this story, I am coming up on nine years of consistent sobriety. When I look back on the journey this far, I honestly can't explain what happened. Something out there had my back—call it a power greater than myself, call it whatever you want. I cannot explain how I went from a Lifetime Convict Scumbag to what many would call a Good Honorable Man who has helped many. Today my life is different. It's a normal life with a loving wife and two kids, a steady job, and a house. But the most important thing I have today is peace. I got high so much because while I was high, I felt a sense of peace. Today I have it without substances.

I am blessed to have been able to take it full circle and be of service to CMA at so many levels and in so many ways. I've been able to go back to every halfway house, detox, jail, and prison I've ever been in. I've been able to go inside as a free man and speak to those who are stuck in those positions. I've been able to give them hope that they can recover, that it doesn't matter what they've done, where they're from, or what they think or feel about themselves.

We can do this, and we can have a good life far beyond our wildest dreams. There are many "convicts" who surround me and with whom I have been able to walk through this journey. Today they are happy, healthy, and doing the right thing: helping others.

As I close out my story, my hope for you is that you find in CMA what I found: hope, fellowship, belonging, and an overall way out of the dark. I highly encourage you to find the fellowship and reach out. We want nothing from you but to see you succeed and have that peace we all desire. Don't let anyone tell you that you can't do this, because you can! I hope you will.

COMING FULL CIRCLE

When I first came into this program, I couldn't stay sober to save my life. I was what they call a chronic relapser, a retread—whatever you want to call me, that's what I was. But this program was always there. Every time I came back all torn up and beat up, they were always ready to welcome me with open arms. Like, "Let's do this again." Never once was I beaten down by others, only by myself.

So, what happened? What was it like? What is it like now? What happened was I love crystal meth. I am a tweaker from back in the '90s. I tried crystal meth for the first time when I was 20.

I got married really young, when I was 17. Now, you know you're doing something wrong when your parents need to sign for you. I got married because I'm Hispanic, and I was pregnant, and my dad was like, "You're getting married." So that's what I did. Before I was even old enough to drink, I had two kids, was married, and was miserable.

When I tried crystal meth for the first time, unfortunately, it was like, "I have arrived!" It was my saving grace. It was that one thing that was just like a free-for-all. But the problem was, I had two kids, and my husband was not having it. He was so not having it. My son was 2 and my daughter was 6 months old. My ex-husband is Hopi Indian, so he took my son and went back to the reservation and left me with my daughter in Phoenix. She was still in one of those carrier things. Anyway, I just couldn't do it. So I left her off at the nursery downtown. I was really going to go back and get her. I really was. But I didn't.

Today, I can tell you, the things I did to my children kept me sick for a really long time. I never allowed myself to be happy. I never allowed myself to smile. I never had any joy, because of what I did to my kids. I hate to tell you this, but I didn't see my daughter again until she was 16, and I didn't see my son until he was 18 or 19.

So it was a long tortuous drug life, the life that goes along with being an addict. It's a really hard life, but I did it, and I did it for a really long time. The problem with me using crystal meth is that I don't know how to do it without getting in trouble, so there were consequences immediately. That meant that I spent a lot of time in jail. I can't even tell you how many times I ended up in the County Jail.

I was one of those who would go in for 10 months here and 6 months there; whatever the time was, I did it. But every time I went in I'd say, "I'm not gonna do this anymore." And if you'd have given me a stack of Bibles, I'd have sworn I meant it with every fiber in my body. "I'm not gonna do this again." I can't tell you how many times I got out and was high the same day. One time I got out of jail after 10 months in the tents, and my boy-friend at the time picked me up in a stolen car. I ended up going back the same day, wearing the same clothes and high as hell.

That was just the way I lived. The Big Book talks about how our addict or alcoholic life is the only one we know. That's just our norm. I'm just gonna die a tweaker, right? And it says, "We are unable, at certain times, to bring into our consciousness with sufficient force the memory of the suffering and humiliation of even a week or a month ago. We are without defense against the first drink." For me, that's like sitting in the back of the police car thinking, *I did it again, here I go again*, and really, really in my heart of hearts, saying, *I'm not gonna do this anymore.* But once I get released and those gates are opened, I can't remember what it was like in that police car, and I can't remember what I was telling myself, or probably even praying, "God please help me," like a foxhole prayer.

The first time I went to prison I did five years, and at that point, right before I went in, I had been on the streets, homeless, for three or four years. I was in Sunnyslope, 5th Avenue and Hatcher, right behind the carnicería; that was my spot. No family, nobody wanted to have anything to do with me. I was just miserable, broken, and lost. So when I got arrested, I knew I was going to prison, and I remember feeling this feeling like, *Just take a break!* I remember thinking, *I'm gonna go do this time, I'm gonna get out, nobody's going to remember me, and I can just start my life over again.*

So here I go. I do my five years in prison, and let me tell you, I'm not proud of it, but I can do some prison time. I did five years and didn't get one ticket. I can be a good little inmate, but when I get out, I really don't know how to act.

I decide if they're going to take five years of my life, I'm going to go to school. So I go to school, and I work in the automotive program for my last three years there and get all these certifications.

I got released and went home to live with my dad and went to work in the automotive field, which I can tell you is a very hard industry to work in for a woman. I stayed sober for a while, not because I had any program. I was just abstinent—I think the fear of going back to prison was my motivating factor.

That year, I met my husband and got married. I had a family, and I wasn't using. But then things got tough for me. We found my 18-year-old niece dead in her bed from a heroin overdose. She had just graduated from high school. It was really tough. That was in February. And right before Father's Day that year, my mom passed away from cancer—she'd been battling it for a long time.

What happened then is "life." And that's the reality of it. Life started to happen. I was on probation, because I left with the tail, and when I didn't know how to deal with life, what I did was pick up and use. I relapsed in July.

My husband is an alcoholic, but he didn't know the life of a tweaker. I dragged him through the mud. He kept saying, "Where are you going? Why are you gone all the time?" I was like, "I want to be the good little housewife and good mom to my stepson, but I want to go smoke meth in the bathroom, or I want to stay out all night and dumpster dive." He couldn't understand that.

Six months later, where am I? I'm in the back of a police car getting busted again. That's the pattern of my life. I'm sitting in the back of the car, and the cops ask, "Who do you want to call?" I said, "I don't care who you call, just do not call my husband." How selfish of me. I'm not coming home after work, and he's going to be worried sick, and I'm just thinking about me and my pride and my ego and I don't want to face this. So selfish! But the guys at the shop called my husband and said, "Hey, your wife's getting arrested."

He gets me out of jail, gets me a lawyer, and the lawyer tells me, "You probably should get some help." For me, getting help means, "Let's go back to prison." That's my rehab, that's my "get straight," my "get clean." My lawyer tells me I should probably check myself into somewhere. And that's what I did. That was my first taste of recovery.

I went to a halfway house. That halfway house was my foundation. It was a sacred place for me. That's where I first developed relationships with women. I started going to meetings and building a network of women around me who were super-genuine. When you're living out on the streets and you're living my life, you don't trust women. They either want your clothes or your boyfriend. But these women were like, "How are you doing?" And they really meant it, they really cared.

I loved it there and took days off from work just to hang out and sit on the patio and smoke cigarettes and talk. Then a couple of days before I got out of there and got my certificate, I went to court, and they gave me what they call a super-mitigated sentence, which is one-tenth of an original sentence.

We go back to prison. I say "we" because my husband ended up living in a "prison," too. I did about seven and a half months, and it was harder than the whole five years I did before. My husband was there every single Saturday. I remember him coming to visitation and thinking, *Man, I got to stop doing this to this guy. He's a good guy, and we got a good life. There's no reason I should be out doing what I was doing and getting high.*

It wasn't until then that I realized I suffer from a disease. I get this obsession, and I get this feeling that I just want more. It's like I have this little guy in my head who tells me I don't deserve this good life. "You know what you want to do, go back and do what you do, 'cause that's what you do good, and all of this is for somebody else. It looks good on them, but not on you." That's what my head tells me.

When I get out of prison this time, I go back to meetings. That's one thing: I never stopped coming back, never stopped walking through those doors and picking up that 24-hour chip so many times. I get sober, I do my Steps in like 60 days, and I'm taking women to meetings and sponsoring a couple of women. I get about a year sober, and I get this great job working in recovery. What people told me not to do is exactly what I did. They said, "Don't make that job your recovery." And that's exactly what I did. I quit going to meetings. I was too busy to take phone calls from sponsees. I hadn't talked to my sponsor in weeks, and I can't even tell you the last time I'd gone to a meeting, because I was too busy.

When you stop having that connection with your Higher Power, you stop praying, you stop doing all those things you did to get your foundation, you lose it, and that's what I did—I lost it. I thought one day that getting loaded was a great idea, and I did.

Trying to work in the field of recovery and getting loaded is the worst feeling I have ever felt in my life—being such a hypocrite and a liar and just dying inside, torturing myself. I did that for a couple of months. My husband kicked me out of the house for three days, and I began living and using in my car. Again, I had no reason why I should be getting loaded, but that obsession to use was back. I woke that monkey up and fed that demon, and I couldn't let him go.

I believe this is when I really had my First Step experience of having every reason in the world not to use, sitting there crying as I'm using, and just not being able to stop. I know I have to, and I want to, but I just can't stop. I lived that agony a good solid two days. I get what they talk about in Step One, being absolutely powerless.

I went to sleep one night and had a dream that I was back in prison standing on the yard looking at the razor wire, knowing that I'm there for a really long time and telling myself, *If you only would have stopped, you wouldn't be here right now.* I woke up the next morning and thought, *Oh, that was just a dream,* and continued using. The next night I had the same dream. I believe in my heart of hearts that God was talking to me, telling me, "If you don't stop using, something bad, bad, bad is going to happen, and there's nothing you can do about it." I woke up the next morning and told my husband, "I'm done!"

I was so full of fear, not just because that dream freaked me out, but because I was so scared that I was never going to use crystal meth again. What is my life going to look like when I really don't ever have to use crystal meth again?

When I told my husband I was done, he said, "You know what you have to do and who you have to call." I called my sponsor and told her I'd been using and she said, "I know." I said, "Why didn't you say anything?" She asked, "Would it have mattered?" She was right. I would have lied. I would have lied right to her face.

I haven't looked back since. I did my Steps again with my sponsor. I really feel I had a First Step experience with those dreams. I believe my Second Step was God talking to me. When we were working on my Third Step, my sponsor said one of my character defects is that I care what people think about me. So she made me pray in public on my knees, and every time I did, I had to take a picture of where I was and send it to her. She said, "It doesn't really matter what anybody thinks. It's none of your business what people think about you."

I dove again into recovery and got busy. But this time I didn't come back to CMA. I went to meetings in another fellowship. I did that because of the guilt and shame over something I had done in my group. I have to share this whenever I speak at a meeting, because it's important to my recovery. This is one of those secrets that we talk about in the Fourth and Fifth Steps. The ones we think we will take to the grave. For me, it was like deny, deny, deny.

When I had a little bit of sobriety and was involved in CMA, I was chairing a meeting. I was the chair, secretary, and the treasurer, and the meeting died. I got loaded and stopped going, so nobody was there to chair it, and the meeting died. I took the money from the meeting. It was $72. I never told anybody, and I never put it on my Fourth Step. I never even told my sponsor.

When I was a few months sober, I went to a CMA convention because somebody asked me to go to a marathon meeting to hear him speak. I crept into this little marathon meeting. I hadn't been to CMA since I'd gotten sober, and I just sat there. All of a sudden, I just felt this overwhelming sense of sadness, and I just started crying at that meeting. There were five or six people there, and they were like, "Why's she crying?"

This guy spoke, everybody shared a little bit, and then people started asking, "Irene, do you want to share?" and I said, "Nope!" They persisted: "We think you really should." I said, "I owe this fellowship an amends." *Oh, my God, I can't believe I just did that,* I thought. I didn't know at the time that the head of security was at the meeting, and he went to get the chair of the convention. I knew this guy, Brian, from before. He's been a huge part of my recovery.

I said, "Brian, I owe this fellowship an amends, I stole money when I chaired a meeting." It was $72, and I had $60 in my pocket, so I asked, "What can I do to make it right?" He said, "We want you back in service; we want you back in this fellowship." And I can tell you I haven't stopped. That was in 2014, and I knew that day, leaving that convention, I was going to be OK. I was really going to be OK.

It wasn't like, "I got this." But I felt this peace inside my heart. I knew that God had me walk through that experience, and the obsession to use has been lifted from me. I don't know if it was that day, but I know I felt a sense of ease and comfort. It was the feeling the Big Book talks about when we first take a drink. I felt this ease and comfort that I'm in the right place where I'm at today in my recovery. I felt a sense of connection to my Higher Power that I never had before.

So what does my life look like today? This past year I got voted to be the chair of this year's convention. And talk about coming full circle: I do a prison meeting every other Saturday, back on the same yard that I rolled out of. I've been jail-badged for two years now. I go every Wednesday and Monday—the same jail! I speak to those women like they are one of me. Other than the color of their clothes, I am them.

The lady I go into the prison with asked me, "Where did you used to sleep?" and I said, "You see that bunk where those two girls are sharing a TV? I slept there for three years." Talk about coming full circle and doing the work this program requires!

I try to talk honestly, from my heart, with these women. I've watched them come in and spend months and months, get out, come back, and do it again. I feel like right now, I'm the solid that they have. I'm always going to be there for them. Even if they get out and they don't call me or I don't see them in a meeting and they come back, I'm always going to be there. They're going to pick the pieces up and do this again.

You know, it's really crazy: I stole that money, I made it right, and I'm making my amends to this fellowship. And wouldn't you know it, for the first year, I'm the treasurer of my group! I'm like, "Do you guys know? Have you heard my story?" They're like,

"That's OK. We already know." I'm honored and grateful they trust me. That's a testament to this program, to this fellowship, to getting that connection with a Higher Power. He carries me on when I feel like there are times I just can't do this anymore.

I'm struggling right now. I have a sister out there doing the most, and I want to save her so bad. But I can't. I can help all these women I don't even know, but I can't even help my sister. It hurts, but I know she's got to have her own experience and not my experience. I just pray for her every single day. I answer the phone. I take her food when she needs it. I don't give her any money, and I just pray for her. Now I understand what my dad went through all those years with me running around and not being in contact with him. I watch the news and hear about a dead body, and I think, *Text my sister and make sure she answers.* I get it now; I totally get it.

I don't ever want to live that life. And if you're new, we do recover! We do have fun! We have fun in this program, trust me. I'm a tweaker, and if I couldn't keep busy and do stuff, I would not stay. I love this program, and I love the people here. CMA rocks!

START A MEETING

VOICES OF THE ®
FELLOWSHIP

Starting a meeting is easy. You just need two or more crystal meth addicts and **a desire to stay clean and sober.**

BRINGING CMA INSIDE A FACILITY

If your facility permits it, you may be able to start your own Crystal Meth Anonymous meeting run totally by facility residents. Everything you need is included in this book.

Starting a CMA meeting is surprisingly simple, and it may be one of the most exciting things you ever do in recovery. One thing we can tell you for certain is that we don't get sober alone.

By reaching out to help—and get support from—other addicts, you can make an enormous difference in not just your own recovery, but also in the lives of other addicts. More good news: Thousands of addicts have gone before you, and we're more than happy to help. We've gathered here some ideas to help you get started, some answers to questions you may have, and some suggestions based on our experience.

At its most basic, a meeting is a group of two or more recovering addicts who get together to help one another stay clean—to carry the message of recovery to each other and, most important, the newcomer. This is the primary purpose of any group.

The most basic type is a group-sharing meeting, where, after some initial readings, members take turns talking about their experience of working the Twelve Steps, other issues they face in recovery, and what is working to help them stay clean. Some meetings choose to focus the sharing by keeping a list of topics or reading a Step or some other bit of recovery literature and asking people to share on that topic. You may let people share randomly as they are moved to.

Choosing a Meeting Type

Here you will find a selection of meeting formats. The readings are suggested; you may choose to use them or have no readings at all. We do, however, suggest that the Twelve Steps be read at every meeting, because these are the basis of the program that changes our lives. Truly, the meeting is the means through which the Steps are introduced to a suffering addict.

Choose one of these formats:

Speaker Meeting
One member shares their experience, strength, and hope with the Twelve Steps of recovery, followed by open sharing if there is time. To avoid war stories and glorifying drug use/criminal behavior, we suggest that the speaker follow the simple format of, what it was like, what happened and what it is like now, as we describe it here.

> What it was like: How did you get into drugs and what was life like as an addict?
>
> What happened: What were the consequences of your using? How did you recognize that you had a problem and how did you find recovery?
>
> What it's like now: What is your life like in recovery? How does the program help you stay sober? What are you looking forward to in the future if you stay sober?

Topic/Discussion
The meeting facilitator chooses a recovery principle (e.g., honesty, hope, faith, courage, integrity, willingness, humility, serenity, acceptance, surrender, spiritual awareness, fellowship, brotherly love, service), and the floor is open to sharing on that topic.

SCRIPT FOR A BASIC FORMAT

Hello, welcome to this meeting of Crystal Meth Anonymous. My name is _____ and I'm an addict. Please help me open this meeting with the Serenity Prayer.

"God, grant me the serenity to accept the things I cannot change, courage to change the things I can, and wisdom to know the difference."

Crystal Meth Anonymous is a fellowship of people for whom all drugs, especially crystal meth, have become a problem. The only requirement for membership is a desire to stay clean and lead a sober life. The fellowship advocates complete abstinence from crystal meth, alcohol, medications not taken as prescribed, and all other mind-altering substances. There are no dues or membership lists, and each group is expected to be self-supporting through its own contributions. The Twelve Steps of CMA are suggested to provide us with a plan with which to build a better, sober life. We believe if we work these simple Steps, we will live a life free of active crystal meth addiction.

This is not meant to embarrass anyone, but so we may get to know you better, would those of you here for the first time please raise your hand and tell us who you are?

I have asked _____ to read **"What Is CMA?"**

I have asked _____ to read **"Are You a Tweaker?"**

I have asked _____ to read **"The 12 Steps: A Plan of Action."**

The format for today's meeting is (Speaker/Discussion or Topic/Discussion).

(For speaker) I have asked _____ to share their story.

(For topic) I have asked _____ to share on a topic.

The meeting is now open for discussion.

We have come to the end of our meeting. I have asked _____ to read **"I Can Stay Sober,"** and take us out with the serenity prayer.

OUR READ- INGS

Our **original CMA Conference-approved literature,** read aloud at our meetings.

WHAT IS CMA?

CMA has a simple message:
Recovery from meth addiction is possible.
You never have to use again.
And you don't have to recover alone.

We are Crystal Meth Anonymous. Together we practice the Twelve Steps as a new way to live, free from crystal meth use.

The only requirement for membership is a desire to stop using. There are no dues or fees. We share our experience, strength, and hope to help each other stay clean and sober, one day at a time. Through our actions and service, we carry the message of recovery to the addict who still suffers.

Our fellowship advocates complete abstinence from crystal meth and all other mind-altering substances, including alcohol, marijuana, inhalants, and any medication not taken as prescribed.

We suggest laying a solid foundation with

- Meetings and fellowship
- Sponsorship and Step work
- Service and commitments

Remaining anonymous gives every member the same opportunity to recover. We are simply addicts helping other addicts.

If you think you have a problem with crystal meth, you're in the right place. You always have a seat here. Welcome home.

ARE YOU
A TWEAKER?

It doesn't matter what you call it. It doesn't matter how you did it. It brought us to our knees, because without exception, that's what it does.

Is speed a problem in your life? Are you an addict? Only you can answer those questions.

For most of us who have admitted defeat, the answer is very clear. Yes, we had a problem with speed, and no, we couldn't fix the problem by ourselves. We had to admit defeat to win. Speed was our master.

We couldn't control our drug use. What started out as weekend or occasional use became daily use, and we soon found ourselves beyond human aid. We truly suffered from a lack of power to fix our problem.

Some of us used speed as a tool to work harder and longer, but we couldn't keep a job. Others picked at their faces and arms for hours and hours or pulled out their hair. Some of us had uncontrollable sexual desire. Others endlessly tinkered with projects, accomplishing nothing, but found ourselves so busy we couldn't get to work on time.

We deluded ourselves into thinking that staying up for nights on end was OK, that our tweaking was under control, and that we could quit if we wanted to, or that we couldn't afford to quit, or that our using didn't affect our lives.

Maybe we saw a friend go to jail, or lose their apartment, or lose their job, or lose the trust of their family, or die, but our clouded minds wouldn't admit we were next.

Most of us saw no way out, believing that we would use until the day we died.

Almost universally, if we had an honest moment, we found that our drug use made seemingly insurmountable problems in our lives.

The only way out was if we had the courage to admit that speed, our one time friend, was killing us.

It doesn't matter how you got here. The courts sent some of us, others came for family or friends, and some of us came to CMA on our own. The question is, if you want help and are willing to go to any lengths to change your life?

THE TWELVE STEPS: A PLAN OF ACTION

We come to CMA because of our common problem. We stay because of our common solution. To find long-term freedom from the grip of addiction, we work the Twelve Steps of Crystal Meth Anonymous:

1. We admitted that we were powerless over crystal meth and our lives had become unmanageable.
2. Came to believe that a power greater than ourselves could restore us to sanity.
3. Made a decision to turn our will and our lives over to the care of a God *of our understanding.*
4. Made a searching and fearless moral inventory of ourselves.
5. Admitted to God, to ourselves and to another human being the exact nature of our wrongs.
6. Were entirely ready to have God remove all these defects of character.
7. Humbly asked God to remove our shortcomings.
8. Made a list of all persons we had harmed and became willing to make amends to them all.
9. Made direct amends to such people wherever possible, except when to do so would injure them or others.
10. Continued to take personal inventory and when we were wrong promptly admitted it.
11. Sought through prayer and meditation to improve our conscious contact with a God *of our understanding* praying only for the knowledge of God's will for us, and the power to carry that out.
12. Having had a spiritual awakening as a result of these steps, we tried to carry this message to crystal meth addicts, and to practice these principles in all of our affairs.

Crystal meth seemed like the answer to our problems. Not anymore. We realize our drug use was killing us. Once we started, we couldn't stop. Today, to stay clean and sober, we don't pick up—no matter what.

When we take action, we choose faith over fear and progress over perfection. As we work the Steps, we put spiritual principles into motion.

Surrender is an action...it brings freedom.
Humility is an action...it brings perspective.
Gratitude is an action...it brings contentment.

This is the gift of recovery: We awaken, our lives improve, and we gradually move from self to service. We act as messengers to others who are suffering—messengers of hope and healing, of connection, compassion, and yes, even joy.

THE TWELVE TRADITIONS OF CRYSTAL METH ANONYMOUS

The Twelve Traditions guide the group just as the Twelve Steps guide the individual.

1. Our common welfare should come first; personal recovery depends on CMA unity.
2. For our group purpose there is but one ultimate authority—a loving God as expressed in our group conscience. Our leaders are but trusted servants; they do not govern.
3. The only requirement for CMA membership is a desire to stop using.
4. Each group should be autonomous except in matters affecting other groups or CMA as a whole.
5. Each group has but one primary purpose—to carry the message to the addict who still suffers.
6. A CMA group ought never endorse, finance, or lend the CMA name to any related facility or outside enterprise, lest problems of money, property, or prestige divert us from our primary purpose.
7. Every CMA group ought to be fully self-supporting, declining outside contributions.
8. Crystal Meth Anonymous should remain forever nonprofessional, but our service centers may employ special workers.
9. CMA, as such, ought never be organized, but we may create service boards or committees directly responsible to those they serve.

10. Crystal Meth Anonymous has no opinion on outside issues; hence the CMA name ought never be drawn into public controversy.
11. Our public relations policy is based on attraction rather than promotion; we need always maintain personal anonymity at the level of press, radio, television, films, and other public media.
12. Anonymity is the spiritual foundation of all our traditions, ever reminding us to place principles before personalities.

I CAN STAY SOBER

I can stay sober.
I don't have to relapse.
I never need to go back out there;
I can stay here—there is a solution.
I can stay here and stop running;
I can stay here and start saying yes to life.
I can find a Higher Power to rely on.
I can find some peace and find out who I really am.
I can make a decision and make some changes.
I can make some new friends—
And make amends to my old ones.
A lot of addicts will go back to using, but I don't have to.
Not if I get a sponsor and get to work.

Take a deep breath...

If I can accept the truth and put away my fantasy,
If I can ask for a little help,
If I can take these suggested Steps,
One day at a time, I will be free.

(Groups may change this reading to the "We" version.)

TODAY I CAN

Let's not forget what we can do this day:

Today I Can...
Draw on the power of honesty. I embrace change and redefine myself. Word by word, deed by deed—I strive to reflect the truth.

Today I Can...
Put down my old habits. Selfishness and hardness give way to an instinct for service. Gratitude now is my rule.

Today I Can...
Appreciate the richness of life by welcoming, sharing, and laughing with another addict. Turning Godward, I find progress and peace.

Today I Can...
Take in a new reality—that in this struggle I am not alone. Many have walked this path before, and I have fellows at my side.

Today...Together...We Can Live in Hope!

THERE IS HOPE

When we came to CMA, we found other crystal meth addicts who recovered from a hopeless state of mind, body, and spirit. They showed us how to live useful and rewarding lives by embracing a simple program of action.

Through the Steps, we let go of our denial and learned to be honest with ourselves. We developed a relationship with a Higher Power of our _own_ conception. We opened up to another addict about our past and asked our Higher Power to remove our character defects.

We cleaned up the wreckage from the tornado of our old life and embarked upon a new course. We found freedom from fear; love replaced our selfishness.

The truth of our new lives is: We now handle difficulties that once compelled us to use crystal meth. We help others in ways we could never do for ourselves. By finding a spiritual basis on which to live, we can _become_ the miracle of recovery that is happening in the rooms of CMA. We lead incredible lives and give hope to the still suffering addict that recovery from crystal meth is truly possible.

FOR MORE INFORMATION

The CMA Hospitals and Institutions Advisory Committee is available to provide more information about CMA and our fellowship. In many cases we also may be able to send literature at no charge to inmates and those in institutions who are unable to get to a CMA meeting. Please note that requests for literature should come from the recipient. Due to the nature of mail flow to and from facilities, and because this is a volunteer-supported service, literature may take 8-12 weeks to arrive.

For further information, please contact CMA at the following:

Web address:
crystalmeth.org
Click on Contact in the top menu.
Select Hospitals & Institutions; a contact form will show up.

CMA National Helpline:
855 METH FREE (855.638.4373)

Mailing address:
CMA General Services
1920 Hillhurst Ave #1315
Los Angeles, CA 90027

Made in the USA
Monee, IL
15 April 2024

56985737R00046